I0170550

YOGA
COLORING IN BOOK FUN

Monica Batiste

monica batiste

Happy

Love

Peace

Rainbow

Batiste

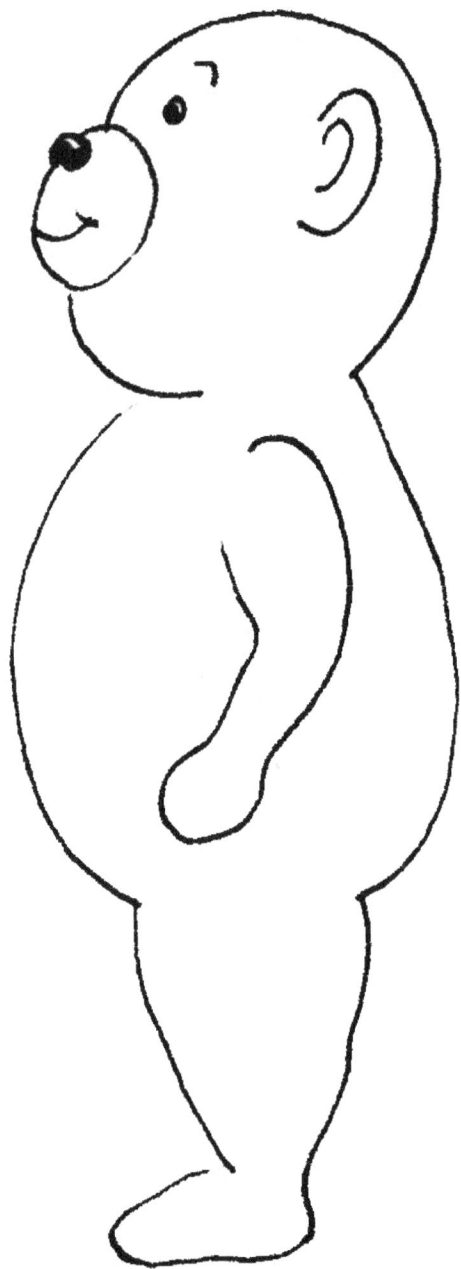

meditation

monica batiste

Monica Batiste

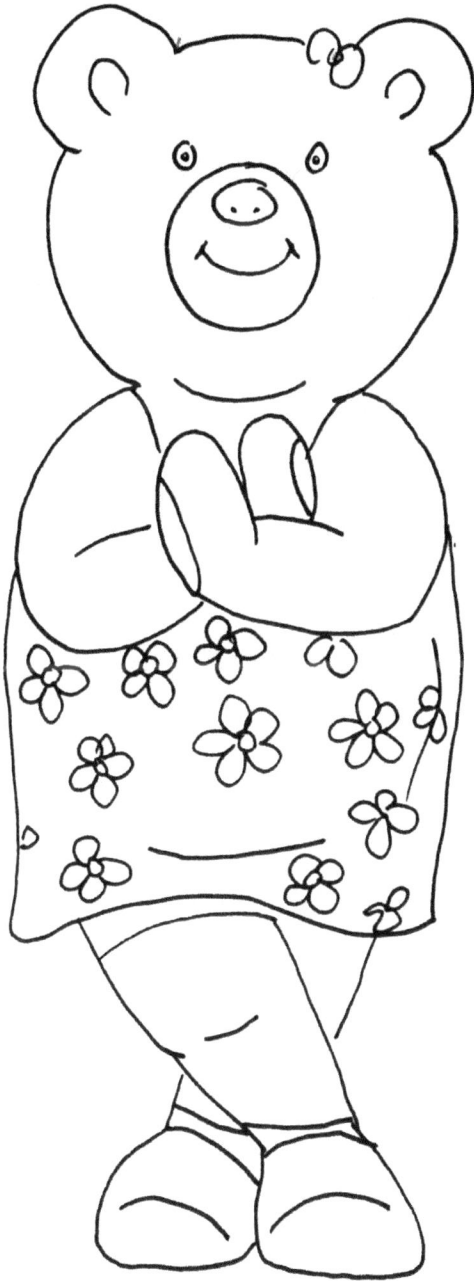

Kindness Respect
Self-esteem
reliable

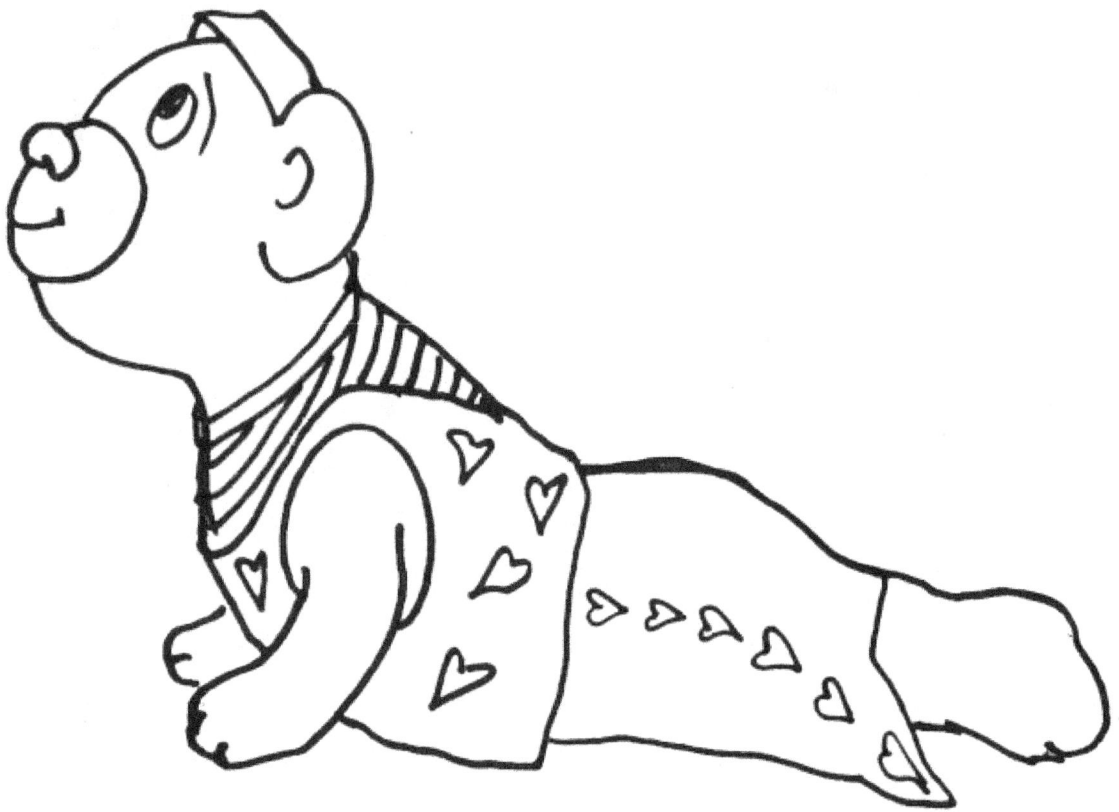

Kindness Award

Kindness Award

Kindness Award

Kindness Award

Kindness Award

Kindness Award

monica batiste

I love honor and approve of me

A Rainbow

Love You You Love You Love

because you are you!
and that is enough

You Love
You Love
You Love
You Love

you are worth it

stretch

life is good

COLOUR ME in

Batiste

Love everyday

I Love ME

Happy Happy Happy me

You are already perfect you are beautiful

I love you

Peace for you

picnics are fun

Love is the best

fun is the best

Happiness is you

You are my Sunshine

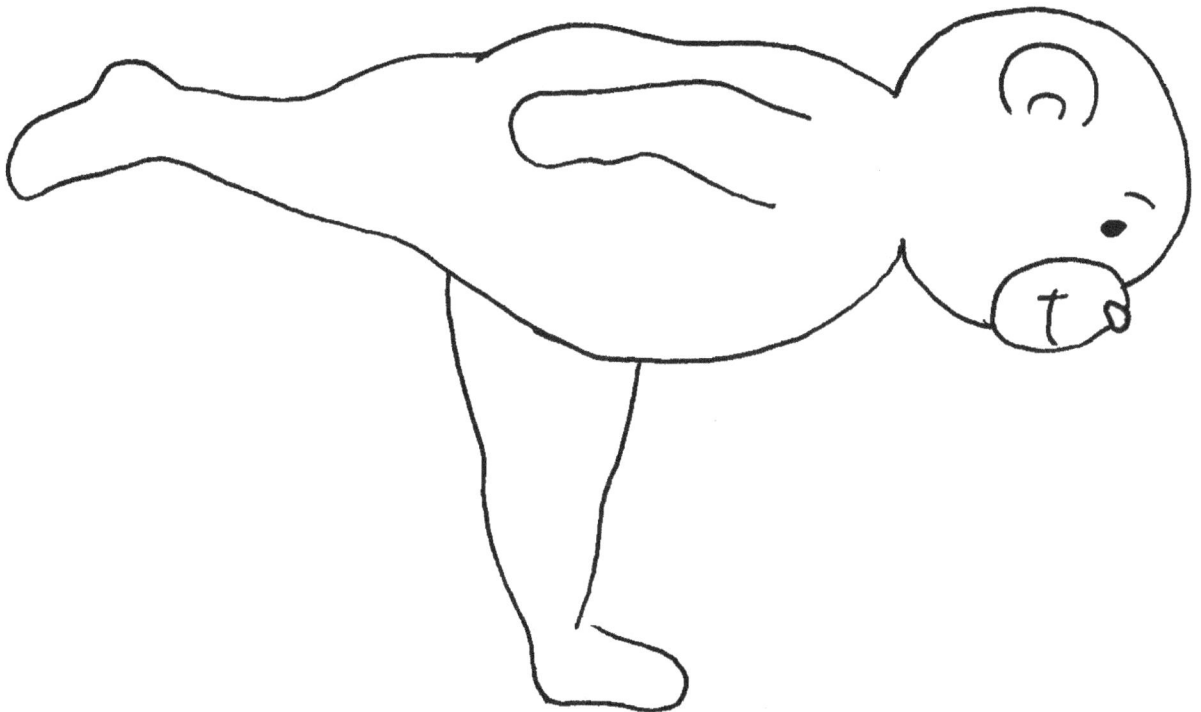

Thank you for buying our Yoga Bear Coloring in Fun book.

Yoga Bear is all about fun, creativity, movement and emotional intelligence.

About Monica
Author, Artist and Teacher

Monica's resources intend to help people grow emotionally, creatively, and to live their best lives.

Monica teaches health, fitness, yoga and art.

If you would like to view more of Monica's books, please visit her website
www.monicabatiste.com.au

Stores at Amazon, Teachers Pay Teachers, and selected book stores.

Contact Monica
info@monicabatiste.com.au
monicabatiste.artist@gmail.com

www.ingramcontent.com/pod-product-compliance
Lightning Source LLC
Chambersburg PA
CBHW081302040426
42452CB00014B/2613